Phyllida Law has appeared in numerous plays, television series and films, including *Peter's Friends*, *Much Ado about Nothing*, *Foyle's War* and *Kingdom*. She was married to Eric Thompson, the writer and narrator of *The Magic Roundabout*, until his death in 1982. She has two daughters, Emma and Sophie.

D0524325

From the reviews of
Notes to my mother-in-law:

'*Notes to my mother-in-law* is something I wolfed in one glorious bite: funny, tender and deeply touching. For anyone who has ever had to look after an elderly relative' ~ Nigel Slater, *Observer* Books of the Year

'A little gem of a book. It is clearly the work of a great natural talker, conjuring for her increasingly ailing relative whole sheaves of hilarious anecdotes. Quickly, they build into a classic of that under-recorded subject: everyday life. There is as much compressed, instinctive humour in these pages as in Alan Bennett's *The Lady in the Van*' ~ Antonia Quirke, *Sunday Times*

'One of the most pleasurable, giddy reads I've had for ages, it's laugh-out-loud funny as well as deeply poignant, illustrated with Law's charming drawings' ~ *Scotsman*

'As extraordinary as the woman who wrote it. The correspondence started with the odd note on the kitchen table reminding Granny Annie of a doctor's appointment or that there was ham in the fridge, but built into more. The result is quite extraordinary. On one level, it's a humorous work about hearing aids and incontinent dogs. On another, it's an uplifting story of family love and duty, and generational conflict' ~ *Daily Mail*

'A life through fridge notes: a strange, particular, grand, funny, touching and remarkable life. Bodily ailments, gruff independence and plain weirdness cause a great character to emerge from the silent end of a dialogue that charms, compels and astonishes' ~ Stephen Fry

'Blissful. Hearing only one side of the conversation between her and Gran makes it as compulsive as eavesdropping on a train, and fifty times funnier. Familiar and inspiring and a reminder to us all that kindness and humour are the best companions in the world' ~ Joanna Lumley

Notes to my mother-in-law

Phyllida Law

FOURTH ESTATE · London

Fourth Estate
An imprint of HarperCollins *Publishers*
77–85 Fulham Palace Road
Hammersmith
London W6 8JB

This Fourth Estate paperback edition published 2011
1

First published in Great Britain by Fourth Estate in 2009

Text and illustrations copyright © Phyllida Law 2009
Except 'How's Gran?' copyright © Emma Thompson 2011 and
'Deluxe in the Gran Stakes' copyright © Sophie Thompson 2011

Phyllida Law asserts the moral right to be identified as the author of this work

A catalogue record for this book is available from the British Library

ISBN 978-0-00-733842-9

Designed and set by seagulls.net

Printed and bound in Great Britain by Clays Ltd, St Ives plc

All rights reserved. No part of this publication may be reproduced,
stored in a retrieval system, or transmitted, in any form or by any means,
electronic, mechanical, photocopying, recording or otherwise,
without the prior permission of the publishers.

This book is sold subject to the condition that it shall not, by way of trade
or otherwise, be lent, re-sold, hired out or otherwise circulated without the
publisher's prior consent in any form of binding or cover other than that in
which it is published and without a similar condition including this
condition being imposed on the subsequent purchaser.

Mixed Sources
Product group from well-managed
forests and other controlled sources
www.fsc.org Cert no. SW-COC-1806
© 1996 Forest Stewardship Council

FSC is a non-profit international organisation established to promote the
responsible management of the world's forests. Products carrying the FSC
label are independently certified to assure consumers that they come
from forests that are managed to meet the social, economic and
ecological needs of present and future generations.

Find out more about HarperCollins and the environment at
www.harpercollins.co.uk/green

For my daughters

PROLOGUE

Annie, my mother-in-law, lived with us for seventeen years and was picture-book perfect.

She washed on Monday, ironed on Tuesday. Wednesday was bedrooms, Thursday baking, Friday fish and floors, Saturday polishing, particularly the brass if it was 'looking red' at her. Sunday was God and sewing. She had a framed print of *The Light of the World* on her bedroom wall and her drawers were full of crochet hooks and knitting needles. She could turn the heel of a sock and the collar of a shirt. She made rock cakes, bread pudding and breast of lamb with barley, and she would open a tin of condensed milk and hide it at the back of the fridge with a spoon in it if things were going badly in our world. She came to us when things had stopped going well in hers.

The rented cottage she left had the rose 'New Dawn' curling over and around a front door she never used. All of life flowed towards the back door and led into the kitchen and her cupboards full of jams and bottled fruit. Her little parlour was all table and dresser, with a fireplace full of wild flowers in a cracked china soup tureen. She wallpapered the front room every spring. Three walls with one pattern and the fourth to contrast. But what she loved most was her wood pile and her long, narrow garden where the hedges were full of old toys and rusty tricycles. Here, my children used to hide on fine summer nights, sitting straight-backed in their flannel pyjamas between rows of beans to eat furry red and gold gooseberries, rasps that weren't ripe and rhubarb dipped into an egg cup of sugar.

All she managed to bring with her to London were two white china oven dishes, half a dozen pocket editions of Shakespeare, her button box, her silver thimble, a wooden darning mushroom, a large bundle of knitting needles tied with tape and a tiny pewter pepper pot, which became a vital prop at our midday planning meetings.

LUNCH.

I have never been able to take lunch seriously, but for Gran it was crucial. She never took anything more than two Rich Tea biscuits and one mug of tea for breakfast, so around noon, depending on her chores, she would say her stomach thought her throat had been cut and come downstairs. When I heard the tap of her wide wedding ring on the banister rail I would strain the potatoes.

The menu was a challenge. I'd learnt from her son that lettuce was 'rabbit food'. (Gran could skin a rabbit as if she was removing its cardigan.) Favourites were fried cheese, Yorkshire pudding, onion gravy, dumplings, stuffed heart and kidneys cooked pink – don't make the plates too hot.

I was nervous. I had discovered garlic. I called baby marrows 'courgettes' and pea pods 'mange-tout'. I ate salad with French dressing, spread marmalade on toasted cheese, and there was no Bisto in the house.

I often feel that food can be as big a stumbler as politics and thought Gran and I might be incompatible in the kitchen – but when lunch was up to scratch her appreciation was so utterly delightful that the meal became a game I loved to win. I planned sudden treats of stale cake – kept cake was more digestible – winkles eaten with a pin or fresh-boiled crab.

Curious about the pretty little pewter pepper pot, I discovered it had come from the Blue Coat School where her father had been a cobbler. Gran had been one of four children, and life couldn't have been easy for she learnt when she was very young how to pawn the candlesticks and bring her mother jugs of beer from the pub.

Her country life began when there was an epidemic of scarlet fever and the Blue Coat School moved out of London. There wasn't enough work so her father was made redundant and Gran went into service at the age of fourteen. She had a scar on one hand from when an irate employer had biffed her with the handle of a broom she had left standing on its bristles. I loved her stories of cruel cooks and horrid housekeepers. It was like having lunch with Catherine Cookson.

Between the juicy bits we organized our days, and it was some while before I realized she was just a bit, as she would say, 'Mutt and Jeff'. It was quite a few years before we all grasped that shouting wasn't enough. After some hilarious misunderstandings, and to avoid confusion, I stuck comprehensive lists on the fridge door beside a large calendar marked with coloured crayons. It still wasn't enough. Gran always said she'd rather be blind than deaf, and aware at last that she was becoming increasingly isolated, I began to write out the day's gossip at the kitchen table, putting my notes by her bed before I went to mine.

One night my husband wandered off to his, muttering darkly that I spent so much time each evening writing to Gran that I could have written a book – 'And illustrated it!' he shouted from the stairs.

Here it is.

Your suspenders were 50p. John Barnes only had pink ones. Got these up Post Office. Change on kitchen table.

———•—•———

The chiropodist is calling at 1.30 p.m. tomorrow (Tuesday). Inconvenient creature. We will have to lunch early and you can have a snooze when he's gone.

———•—•———

Dad is golfing tomorrow. Emma is going to spend the day at the library. I think Sophie and

9

I should be home about teatime. Lamb stew on stove. Kettle on about quarter to five? Ta.

———

Dear, I honestly don't think they would make a mistake like that. They only took a wax impression of the deaf ear, and that must be the one you are meant to put it in I think. Why not try Vaseline? I don't think licking it is a good idea.

———

I'll get some pearl-barley tomorrow, Gran. Sorry about that, the kids hate it, you see. It's a bit slimy. I suppose it *is* very good for you. There was a woman in Ardentinny who used to boil it and strain it and drink the water from it every day. I think she had something wrong with her kidneys.

———

The piano tuner is coming tomorrow at 3 p.m. so when you are dusting don't bother to put back the photos as such. He usually moves everything himself but I'm not sure if he can see terribly well. He seems never to look me straight in the eye and there is something odd about his glasses. It would be awful if he dropped Churchill. Let's give him the last of the rock-cakes. I'll be home so there is no need to stay downstairs for the bell.

———•———

Dusters aren't all that expensive. Perhaps we could use that stockingette stuff the butcher sells? Don't sacrifice your bloomers in this rash manner. Heaven knows where we'll get inter-locking cotton now Pontings is closed. I might try that haberdasher's next to Woolworths in Hampstead. She still keeps those skeins of plaited darning wool. Last time I was in she told me she was one of the first sales ladies in John Lewis. Apparently they lived over the shop in those days in some sort of hostel, which was very strictly run. She got something like 17/6 per week, I think. You probably got that for a year.

———

Listen, we must practise. That Mr Parnes said we must. Ten minutes every day in a carpeted room, he said. Preferably with curtains. So I will come upstairs with your tea tomorrow and we will have ten minutes' practice in your room. The kitchen is far too noisy.

I have to sit *directly* opposite you and speak slowly. As soon as you get used to my voice I'll send someone else up with tea and we'll do a few minutes longer each day. It is essential that we go about this sensibly.

You may have to hold it in your ear for the moment and I'll ring Mr Parnes about other fitting arrangements. He agrees that the main disadvantage is the tiny switch. The tips of one's fingers do go dead after a certain age and how one is supposed to adjust the beastly thing when there is no feeling in one's fingers I can't think.

I'll mark the little wheel thing with a biro when you feel it's about right and we can adjust it before you put it in. That's settled. Practice will commence at 5 p.m. precisely tomorrow, Wednesday 9th inst., 1978.

Thank you very much, Gran. I will go round to Kingston's tomorrow as they close Thursday afternoon. Is it collar you want? Or is it slipper? Green or smoked? Middle gammon is something like 84p per lb. It'll be a great help to have something to cut cold on Saturday.

I found your splint in the hall drawer.

I tell you what I suggest. Just give up knitting for a while and see if that doesn't help. The physiotherapist I went to for my shoulders thought knitting was really bad for you. Especially with aluminium needles. Aluminium gets a very bad press these days. Mother has changed to enamel because she thinks Uncle Arthur is going potty. She says if you put cold water in a hot aluminium pan it pits the metal and you are swallowing chemicals with every mouthful. She says Aunt Avril used to put bicarbonate in with rhubarb and cabbage and an evil green slime used to rise to the top, which was poisonous. And that's what's the matter with Uncle Arthur. I could suggest a few other things.

———

I didn't know Aunt Min was deaf. I thought she just had diabetes. You must ask her how she gets on with the NHS box model. Maybe the knobs

Uncle Arthur

are bigger. Let me put a new battery in for you. They are such wretched fiddly little things and apparently it's only too easy to leave them switched on when not in use. Mr Parnes says one should last you six weeks, but you could have left it on overnight, and that would explain the difficulty. I had a deaf landlady when I was a student and she was forever leaving her apparatus on, when it would give piercing shrieks and she couldn't hear and we would all have to look for the box. It was nearly as big as a wireless.

If there was a thunderstorm she used to unplug herself, cover all the mirrors with dish-cloths and shut herself in the larder under the stairs. Nice woman.

Now, don't forget to make a list of worries for Mr Parnes and we will sort them all out on Friday morning. I'm afraid your routine will be very much disturbed. Let's do the floors on Saturday and the brass before we go on Friday. Variety is the slice of life, as Aunt Avril used to say.

We used the wooden knitting needles for propping up the house-plants. Remember?

———•———

Nothing much of note to report. This weather will kill us all. Take an extra pill. Be a devil. Called on Mrs Wilson as I passed to check on her wrist. She broke it on Tuesday, did I tell you? She tripped on one of those proud paving stones opposite number 48, and in order to stop herself from falling she put out her hand to steady herself against one of the lime trees.

'It just snapped like a twig,' she said.

Being Mrs Wilson, she clattered on up the road and did the shopping before stumbling back home with a wrist like a whoopee cushion. The doctor showed her the X-ray. She says it looked like a crushed digestive biscuit.

'I'm sorry to have to tell you, Mrs Wilson,' he said, 'that you will never have a normal wrist again.'

'My dear,' said Mrs Wilson, clutching my arm, 'I'm deformed.'

Boot has been sick under the hall table.

———·—·———

All set for tomorrow, then? We should leave by 10.30 a.m. so we'll have to forget the brass this week. It seems very early to leave for a twelve o'clock appointment but I'm worried about the parking. Gloucester Place is one way and tremendously long as streets go, which means we'll have to go right down Baker Street to turn into it and cruise along trying to find the right number. Let's hope it's not raining but the forecast is frightful. I think the brolly is in the car.

I'll try to park as close to the house as possible, of course, but what we will have to do is to stop the car by the door and see you inside. Then, while you sit in the waiting room for a bit, I'll park the car comfortably and come back to go in with you. We should have hankies in handbags and some wine gums. Also a biro for the Daily Mail crossword in case we are kept waiting. Most importantly, do not forget the

box with deaf-aid, batteries old and new, and the grotty earpiece. Any change you have in your purse will likely come in handy. I think we'll need two-bob bits for the meter. Lots of them.

I plan to make a slight detour on the way home to pick up fish and chips.

Apparently if I fill in the bit on the back with all the extenuating circumstances I may not have to pay so hang on to your pension for now, darling.

The wee warden was very stricken. He would never have given us one if we'd got there in time but he was writing it out when I arrived, and once they've started they can't stop. They have to complete the beastly thing, you see, because it's numbered and in triplicate or whatever and he can't destroy it, or the Authorities would run him over or something. He's written our story on the back of this piece and I'm to do the same with mine and they will review the situation. He says we might get away with it and we are to apply for one of those orange disabled badges. This means a visit to the doctor and the town hall where apparently they look at you in case you're a fraud. We'll do it. Then we'll park on yellow lines and block bus lanes.

———

Our Mr Parnes is ex-RAF, did you know?

Could you hear him or were you just pretending? You said, 'Yes,' a lot.

I suspect him of speaking quietly to test your apparatus.

He says you mustn't wash it, darling. No harm done apparently but the battery had to be replaced again. Do you remember when I washed the coffee-grinder and wrecked the engine?

We'll start the Waxol treatment tonight. He says we should use it for a week each month and I will check the earpiece with cotton-wool and a toothpick.

Mr P put a biro mark on the earpiece and it's miles further up the wheel so it's nearly at full blast and I am going to fix it with some sticky tape as I think it is liable to slip. There is just a possibility that we may have to pad one leg of your specs.

Maybe it was a bit silly of us to leave it on in the car. It was Mr P's idea but then he probably doesn't drive a Volkswagen. The plan is to train your ears again to accept different levels of sound. We'll start in the garden with the birds and *progress* to washing-machines and Hoovers.

I notice that when he plays selected noises on his machine you seem to nod more often at the treble end of the scale, which accounts for the fact that you can still hear me calling you for lunch.

Also, I thought he was reassuring and sensible on the subject of nerves. Apparently that's why you hear the first words of a sentence and then everything fades. You have always said it was fright that stops you hearing Fred on the phone. 'Hello' is fine and then it's pure panic. It's the ability to *relax* and *concentrate* at the same time, which is needed here. Good training for tight-rope walking. I always do deep-breathing when I'm nervous.

It was a terrific help in my driving test but God knows what it would do to a telephone conversation.

———•——

Everything is easier in a familiar place with a familiar face. Then you can sit and relax and we must sit directly in front of you and in a good light. If you can't see someone it's very difficult to hear them.

Mrs Wilson says that's why the minister is difficult to hear, and he will put his hand over his mouth. Mind you, he is a bit deaf himself, the church echoes and his microphone is faulty.

Mrs Wilson says Mr Wilson is getting deaf and she is trying to keep it from him. You are not alone. Beethoven was deaf. Did you know that? Stoners. Deaf and German. What a disaster. Quite a lot of musicians go deaf. Perhaps you think that's not so surprising.

I'm sorry the drops hurt but I think we must persevere. I'm sure the crackling noise is the wax dissolving and moving about. I'll warm the bottle tonight. Then you can put a little bit of cotton-wool in your ear to hold it in.

Mother rang to say that Mrs Lees is laid up. She was painting the ceiling in the bathroom and she got on to a chair in the bath to do it. Makes me dizzy to think about it. Paint every-where and severe bruising.

No, not gardening. I was burying the contents of the Hoover.

Eleanor said I was to dig a trench for the sweet-peas very early on and fill it with anything I could find. Sweet-peas are gross feeders, she said. I hope they like carpet fluff, hair and bits of old Boot.

The gunge was everywhere. I took the Hoover into the yard, plugged it in with the bag off and gave some sparrows a very violent dustbath.

I remember Aunt Ella once used her Hoover like that to dry her hair. Unfortunately she used egg whites as a conditioner. She used to rinse them off with vinegar or camomile tea to bring up the colour. (She had glorious auburn curls.) Anyway she still had the egg whites on when she bent over to switch the Hoover on and test the air-flow so she ended up with what looked like a grey fur bathing cap. We were enchanted.

Her beauty tips were legion. She used to wrap bits of lint soaked in witch-hazel and iced water round old shoe trees – the kind with a wooden toe at one end, a knob at the other and waggly metal in between – and then she would sit biffing her double chins with the padded toe and saying, 'QX, QX, QX.' Wonderful woman.

So, anyway, I've buried it all. I expect the minister's cats will dig it all up. No sooner do I turn fresh earth up than they all waltz in and pee. He has four, you know, and I saw the big ginger one with feathers sticking out of its mouth. There's a fiendish wall-eyed tom from the flats who dug up all my hyacinths and the banana skins under our roses.

the ministers cat

Mother's neighbour at Ardentinny went all round the coast to pick up a dead rat found on the beach so that she could bury it under her rosebed. They'll eat anything, she says. Roses, that is.

I tipped your button box on to the Times to search for curtain hooks. Found plastic *and* brass. You know, it's an historic collection. There's that big green button which belonged to the first coat we bought you at C & A's. You were horrified by the price but it was a great success. Where the hell is it? Did we leave it in Scotland?

Soph came in and started a personal treasure hunt. She has chosen eight different coloured buttons and is presently cutting off the ones on her pink cardigan to replace them with this rainbow set.

Good grief.

———— ·•· ————

Don't, whatever you do, put your hands into the water in the sink in the washroom. I've got pieces off the stove soaking in a strong solution of Flash. It would play hell with your psoriasis.

I will do the fridge and oven in the morning and clean under the bath. Must get bulk buy of bicarb. I gave Eleanor our last packet for her cystitis so I'll use the box for your teeth and replace it, if you don't mind?

———

I couldn't get Garibaldi biscuits up at Flax's and I couldn't get Min cream. Mrs Venning says it seems to have disappeared off the shelves.

Met Mr Wilson up the hill today and stopped to ask after Mrs Wilson's wrist. She is doing very well but of course he has to do the shopping for her and it hurts his poor feet. Anyway, we were happily passing the time of day when I noticed he had a little flower petal stuck to his cheek. So, without thinking, I put my hand up and picked it off. My dear, it was only a piece of pink toilet paper he'd stuck on a shaving cut. I was mortified.

Talking of toilet paper, I got much the cheapest buy at the International. Quite pleased with myself, and then I had to pay a fine on the library books. They won't let you off if you are an OAP. They say they might if there were 'special circumstances'. They say they are human.

Which reminds me, I've had to pay that parking fine after all. Don't you think that's MEAN?

<hr />

Got Garibaldis at the International.

I know what it is, Gran. It's Boot. She *will* eat spiders. Every so often she has an overdose and throws up on your bedcovers. It's all arms and legs. I think she eats daddy-long-legs as well. It'll be easy to wash out and we can freshen it up outside on the first fine day.

I hoovered under our bed this morning by the way. Found the following: one sock, seven pence, a dod of makeup-covered cotton-wool, two golf tees, one biro and a cardboard box of curtain rings.

———————

Well, I don't understand it. She seems all right generally, doesn't she?

When she howls like that I can't bear it. I've put a bundle of old Daily Mails in the broom cupboard so if she starts yelling try to get one under her.

She's taken all the polish off the parquet in the hall and there is an ugly stain on the tiles under the kitchen table, which I just can't shift. I dread her throwing up on the carpet. We will never get the smell out. Every time the car gets hot there it is again. The unmistakable Boot pong.

Actually I apologised to Mrs Wilson when I gave her a lift the other day and the smell turned out to be some Charentais melon she had in her shopping bag.

———•———

Drops for the last time tomorrow morning. We mustn't forget to ask the doctor about the form for a disabled badge. He has to sign it.

Appointment 5.20 p.m. We'll leave on the hour.

Actually, before we leave let's write down anything you want to ask the doctor. We mustn't waste our visit. All my symptoms fly out of the window as soon as I'm in the door.

Have you enough ointment?

Have you enough pills?

Are you still worried about your eyes?

Do you need any sweeties?

We can pass the sweet shop as we come home.

Mrs Estherson says we won't get coconut logs any more because the Scottish firm of Ferguson's in Glasgow has closed down. She says she thinks she can get us Richmond Assorted.

Mother sends love. She says the ferry was off last week because a jellyfish got stuck in the works.

———

Well done, darling. Thank Heaven that's over, and I expect you'll feel the benefit tomorrow. He says there is no infection whatsoever and just a tiny bit of inflammation from the wax. Keep a wee bit of warm cotton-wool in it overnight. He says it won't affect your aid, and you can go on using it safely. Apparently the wax has absolutely nothing to do with it.

Also, it's natural for syringing to make you feel dizzy and a bit seedy. And it's natural to be scared. He wondered if you ought to have a blood test you looked so pale but I knew it was terror. Also I don't think the water was warm and he was so enthusiastic that he squirted it all over his suit. Serves him right, I say. Never mind, it needed doing. I held the kidney bowl under your ear and it was spectacular. Reminded me we ought to get the chimney swept this year.

While you were recovering there I asked him about deaf-aids and he agreed immediately to an appointment for you at the Royal Free. He says the box models are much easier for elderly people to manage because the controls are larger. It's just circulation, I think. He thought we could stitch a pocket to your pinny on the bodice somewhere so the box wasn't under the table when you sat down, but I think that would muffle the microphone. He said he would certainly sign a form for our disabled badge. He doesn't keep them. You can pick them up at the town hall, he says.

We are getting one! When we get one I can *drive* you to the doctor's and we can park in the Finchley Road, which means we won't have to gallop across the road like that. Those traffic lights don't give us half enough time to cross, do they? I remember I used to find that with the pram.

Oh, and by the way, he has had a very good wheeze about your pills. You can get the same medicine in *liquid* form, and he says he has an idea it works quicker. It must take ages for those depth-charges to dissolve in your stomach. No more choking them down or struggling to halve them.

The doctor said those large pills should be easier to swallow but Mother says Uncle Arthur keeps a hammer in his bedroom to smash his into little bits. He has trouble with his oesophagus, though. Not sure I've spelt that correctly.

Uncle Arthur advancing
on a large pill

The vet says it's fur ball. Why should she suddenly get fur ball? I didn't know ordinary black bring-you-luck type cats ever got fur ball. I thought it was only those fluffy Persian people. In fact, Dad and I paid £3 for a tiny bad-tempered Persian kitten from that pet shop in Parkway when something about the lecture we had on fur ball made us go back for a refund and buy Ms Boot, who was only thirty bob.

Oh, well. Change of life, I suppose. Apparently we have to brush her regularly. She is to be given a dose of liquid paraffin every day for a week, and then once a week as a general rule. Good grief. She seems quite to enjoy the brushing if it's not too near her old scar but I don't know how to get her to take the paraffin. I put one lot in her milk and she stepped in it.

I rang the vet and he says to squeeze her jaws at the corner when she will be forced to grin and then someone can fling it down on a teaspoon. Not much success so far. We've put the liquid paraffin in the cupboard above the fireplace by the way in case we get into a muddle – tho', mind you, Mother used to use it for cooking during the war. She made a wonderful orange sponge with it when we were short of fat. Everyone loved it and it was beautifully light and airy so her cousin Joan ordered one for her baby's christening, and all the baby guests loved it too, with very unfortunate results.

Funny to think of those days. It was 2 oz butter per person per week, wasn't it? When we were staying at Granny's Flora, the maid, would put our butter ration on little dishes by our places so as to be strictly fair, but Granny used to steal bits and give it to Major Reddick, an officer who was billeted on her, and whom she adored. Us kids loathed him. He used to take his teeth out before a meal, wrap them in his khaki hanky and keep them in his pocket till he was finished, when he would replace the teeth and dry his hanky before the fire.

Frightful creature. Flora said he wore a corset. Every morning after breakfast he would rise from the table and say, without fail, 'Let's see what the King has got for us to do today.' Mother says he attacked her in the morning room and she told him she would scream for Mama.

'What's the matter with you?' he said. 'Don't you like men?'

I think uniforms are bad for people.

———————

Darling, we are all terribly sorry. Truly.

I absolutely promise we were not laughing at you, and it was all my fault. Well, it was my fault originally but then Dad started making cheeky remarks and we all got hysterical.

What happened was this: everyone was discussing the merits of bran for constipation. Dad said he knew you hadn't been, but I wasn't constipated, was I, so why did I take it?

So I said, 'Piles.' Well, you know I get piles sometimes, don't you? They started with Emma. Haven't had them for ages but I take bran every day in case. It's quite fashionable.

So then I told them a dreadful story I have never told anyone before.

Last summer, when you and I were visiting Mother, I was suddenly painfully afflicted, and there was no bran in the house. Uncle Arthur won't tolerate it. Mother has tried to give him All Bran for breakfast but he just sits there with bits sticking out of his mouth like a bad-tempered bird building a nest. So, anyway, I had read somewhere that a very good remedy was to put a clove of garlic up your bum. So I did. For about a week – well, every night for about a week. The trick is to get rid of it in the morning, but on the day we drove back south I didn't have time to go to the loo properly and the garlic was still up there, if you see what I mean.

Uncle Arthur & ALL-BRAN

Well, we left very early to catch the first ferry and round about the Lake District with no windows open I'm afraid I was forced to fart and the smell was simply frightful. You were very alarmed and thought there was something wrong with the car. I told you we were passing through farmland and it was probably chemical fertiliser.

Of course, when I was telling this disgusting tale, everyone looked at you and fell about. Do you see? I know you thought we were laughing at *you*, but really we were laughing at *me* and I somehow couldn't get you to hear and Dad was being very wicked and making matters worse.

Please forgive me. I hope you believe we would never talk about you to your face and laugh like that. It's just so impossible when there are a lot of people at table to persuade everyone to talk one at a time and of course your box picks up all the cutlery noise.

It must be horrible for you. I am so sorry. We'd all hate it if you didn't come down to meals, darling. Please don't do that.

———

Mrs Wilson is fine now, but a bit stiff. Mr Wilson drove to Glastonbury last week and brought her back some Holy Water in a petrol can.

She is keen to stick her wrist in that shrine somewhere near Sidmouth. There's a sort of hole in a bit of stone and you put the injured limb through it and pray to some saint. Saint Monica or somebody, it could be. Anyway, it's a woman.

———

Gran, have you seen a set of keys anywhere?

———

Not *this* Tuesday, darling. Next Tuesday. Sorry, sorry, sorry. It was Sunday when I said it and I meant not this Tuesday coming but next Tuesday, i.e. the Tuesday in the week following next Sunday. Oh, curses, it's one of those misunderstandings like the pronunciation of 'scone', and whether a crumpet is a big flat dark thing with holes in it or a wee fat white thing with holes in it, or whether treacle is syrup or the other way round or neither. How long were you sitting with your feet in a bowl?

Mother is in a frantic state. You know the stray cat I told you about? Well, not only did it give Uncle Arthur asthma but it started to get some sort of discharge from its ears so she took it to the vet and he advised her to have it put down. He said it would be kinder to do it at once so she left it with him and came home. Now, of course, Ada tells her that the doctor has lost his tabby and is searching the coast. My dear, she may have murdered the doctor's cat.

Nothing to report.

Dad used some of your psoriasis cream on that rough patch on his shin and it's gone. Brilliant.

The minister's wife came home from a late Thursday bulk shopping trip and dropped a bottle of whisky and six eggs while unloading.

No, nobody was hurt. It's just that whisky costs £6.98.

the whisky cost £6.98

43

Hi, Gran! The doorbell will ring between 2 and 2.30 p.m. Don't be alarmed, it's only Mr Venning come to change the lock. If you have your nap in the chair in the kitchen after lunch you will hear the bell and no bother. I've told Syd he must wait awhile for you to answer so don't rush to the door whatever you do. Absolutely no need.

I've told Gerry just to leave my order on the window-sill, well wrapped against Boot, but she never uses the letter-box now. Not since that day she got stuck. (I remember one holiday in Skye Mother put a Queen of Puddings on the window ledge and a sheep ate the lot!)

Talking of which, lunch is on the stove. Plus lots of rice pudding with a dod of jam (yours).

I shall be home by 4.30 at the very latest, which gives us ample time to get to the doctor at 5 p.m. Your raincoat is on the hallstand. Looks like we'll need it. The kids will have tea mashed by the time we get back.

So it was Mr Venning who finished the rock-cakes! You'll have to make more as I'm hoping against hope that the window-cleaner will come next week.

Nice that Syd had some tea. That was a very good move. Mrs Venning told me about the rock-cakes when I was in to get Brillo Clear-away for the bath. She says Syd has a very sweet tooth. He gave her 50p to go to Alexis for a piece of cheesecake and two Bath buns for his lunch. Well, my dear, she only got a *small* piece of cheesecake for the money. 'Where are the buns?' cried Syd.

'He lives in the past,' says Mrs V.

She tells me old Mr Samuel's grocery is opening shortly as a centre for water beds. I ask you. I expect kids will go in and wreck the place with a packet of pins. Mrs V is highly amused.

Syd says the crack above your door is because all the houses are slipping downhill. And, of course, so is the roof, and the plumbing is original. 'Never mind,' said Mrs Venning. 'You're sitting on a fortune, Mrs T.'

———··———

Escott's are coming to turn the stair carpet on Wednesday week. That's a week this coming Wednesday. Dad has nailed down that waggly stair-rod for safety and they will do it properly when they come. Mr E says we could never do it ourselves and there are three steps which are dangerously threadbare so take care just now.

You will be pleased to hear that I have found bits of carpet in the stair cupboard. How apt. They were behind the boxes of Carnation milk and sugar that Dad bought against famine. Do you remember when things were short in the shops a year or so ago? There was a spate of panic buying. Someone in Japan got crushed to death queuing for toilet rolls, and sugar was rationed for a spell here. Someone punched the manager at Cullen's.

———·———

Wash day again. Time flies. I will do fridge and disgusting oven in the morning. Must get another packet of bicarb.

———·———

Sophie has gone out to meet Beattie and was so late leaving she asked me to tell you she was sorry not to see you.

I was rather relieved. On her top half she was wearing a T-shirt in blotchy eau-de-nil and her denim pea jacket with the badges. Bottom half was sandals and a white cotton petticoat. She looked as if something frightful had happened when she was half dressed and she'd dropped everything and rushed out. I told her she might be a bit chilly from the waist down and she said she got an A in Art.

She has left three gnawed spare ribs on the kitchen table, which she had put in her bag at the restaurant last night to give to somebody's dog. I don't know whose dog. They weren't even her spare ribs.

———•———

Herewith:

- bottle of Gee's Linctus
- some Shield tablets
- wine gums
- Bourbon biscuits

Of course you can't hear anything – you've got cotton-wool in your ears.

Bit worried about Boot. Does she still meet you in the morning as usual? That strange third eyelid seems to be a bit stuck on her left eye.

———————

Eleanor is much better. She rang me today. She is consumed with guilt about Mother's birthday. She sent a letter, and a parcel was to follow but her local PO was broken into the afternoon of the day she posted it. Men with guns. And it's a tiny place, she says. The sort that keeps dog biscuits in the window. The owner has shut up for a few days to recover. Eleanor says he looks awfully ill. Meanwhile the parcel is either still sitting there or the gunmen have got away with lavender talcum powder, some after-dinner mints and a tin of truffles.

———•———

I've found the keys. They were in the bottom of my wardrobe. Can you beat it? I had to sit down for a minute. What I think must have happened is that I hung up my cleaning holding the bunch of keys and let them go as all the hangers were put in place. Of course, the bottom of our wardrobe is full of shoes and scarves and old plastic bags and aprons so I didn't hear them fall. I might never have found them. But they're no use now and X pounds down the drain.

I am a dizzy tart. It runs in the family. Mother lost a pair of tights she'd bought in Dunoon and rang the shop fussing and furious only to find them in the fridge. There was one wet winter when she put her shoes to dry in the bottom oven of the Rayburn and forgot for weeks. Dinky little stone shoes they were.

No, I won't tell you how much. Put your pension to better use.

No, darling, I don't think there is any question of your having a cataract. I think that some of those library books have very small print, and the doctor feels the mistiness is to do with your general health, but we'll check at the op-thingummy.

You can see a cataract. My granny's was very noticeable.

I don't know why Aunt Min can't get hers done. Perhaps it's because of her diabetes? It's as simple nowadays as a tonsillectomy but I remember Granny's was a grand affair when you lay bandaged in a darkened room for ages. Of course, Granny refused. She got up immediately and wandered about the ward in her flannel nightie removing everyone's bandages as well as her own. In the end they sent her home for bad behaviour. Mother always says she got into an old gentleman's bed, but

I don't think the old gentleman was there at the time.

We had to ban Granny as a subject of conversation because she was so appalling everyone wanted to know about her latest iniquity and other concerns were elbowed.

Do you know, she used to turn the electricity off at the mains if she felt people had overstayed their welcome. And when we had a visitor I would be sent upstairs to light the gas fire in their bedroom (the house was always freezing). When I'd done it I'd slide under the bed until I saw Granny's little black shoes tip-tapping to the fire to switch it off. Satisfied and breathing heavily, she would trot away to her room and I would emerge to relight the fire. She must have been ninety. My brother said she would live for ever because she ate all the mould off the top of the jam pots. My other job was to hide behind the curtains in the dining room to collect the dirty plates she carefully put away.

She called it 'clean dirt' as she wiped them with a licked finger.

She put great faith in *spit*. I was about six when I fell heavily on a cinder path and a little cinder embedded itself in my forehead. Granny cleaned it up and spat on the wound. 'There now,' she said. 'That'll heal over nicely.' And it did. I had to go to the doctor's to have the cinder dug out. You can see the dent in my forehead to this day.

going to church

Around this time Gran had the first of her many falls. I found her on the loo floor with one little foot in its size-three shoe wedged around the lavatory pedestal. I couldn't pick her up because she was laughing so much. Eventually I managed to pull her into a sitting position and give her a cup of sweet tea.

'Oh, thank heaven I've *been*,' she said, hiccuping.

When I finally had her upright I walked her to her bedroom by placing her feet on my size fives, like you do with kids, and we swayed shrieking across the landing, counting loudly at each uncertain step.

This was when I learnt that severe bruising is more painful than a break, or so the doctor said. Bed rest was prescribed. We rigged up a commode on a dining chair with a Wedgewood tureen shaped like a cabbage beneath it. It sold at auction for quite a lot some time later.

Mother sends acres of healing love. She says she fell down the manse stairs with her portable wireless in one hand and her tea in the other so she knows how you feel.

Uncle Arthur is pretty well, considering. Ma got up the other morning very early and feeling chilly, only to find him kneeling at his open window and just wearing his pyjama jacket. She thought he was dead or praying but he was taking aim at a rabbit. He keeps a shotgun under his wardrobe. Mill's pet rabbit used to eat the sitting-room carpet. It had to have a hysterectomy and, appalled by its pain, she fed it port and Veganin. Killed it. She couldn't understand it because her monkey was an alcoholic. They all are, I'm told. When she took him to the pub, folk would ask what her little friend fancied. Port-and-brandy was his favourite.

The girls will serve tea in your boudoir at 4 p.m. or thereabouts. You are getting better, I can tell.

Matron

———

I got the Baby Bio. It's underneath the sink. Treated myself to a can of Leaf Shine (very expensive). The flipping tobacco plant I got from Molly gets me down. Can I rip off that yellow leaf now?

I've washed the fanlight at the front door and emptied the bluebottles out of the lamp-shade. What's more, I've given the door itself a coat of linseed oil because I found half a bottle in the hall cupboard. Used the paint-brush Dad ruined creosoting the deckchairs.

Very successful. The linseed oil has softened the bristles. Also, which is good news, the holes in the panelling are not woodworm but marks from the drawing pins we used to put up the wreath at Christmas. Ha!

———·—

Mrs Wilson sends love. Her arthritis is being kept at bay with some injection or other. Do you fancy a go?

Mr Wilson fell down the tube-station stairs at Trafalgar Square last week and 'came to' in the Middlesex. He has a lump on his head the size of a cricket ball and the bruise is slipping down his face. Mrs W says he may have to have it lanced.

Dr P says you might think about getting up and sitting in your chair tomorrow afternoon.

The girls will re-open lessons with 'the Box'.

Normal service should resume on Monday.

Coming down the hill from the cleaners I saw Larry T on his front steps with a dustpan and brush, wearing yellow rubber Marigold gloves. He was about to clear up the corpse of a rat that had walked up the stairs, looked at him piteously and died on his doormat.

I had a friend who was having a bath when a rat came out of the loo, collected a bar of soap and went back down. She keeps the complete works of Shakespeare and a huge family Bible on the loo lid in between times. The rat apparently lived in the flat below where it ate a cardboard carton full of tampons, and built a brilliantly comfortable nest with the contents. They are clever creatures. Mr Richardson used to keep pet rats. They used to sit on his chest and nibble sugar off his moustache.

Shall I leave Boot in your room tonight?

Darling, do try not to worry about it. I'm sure that's part of the problem. Any sort of tension or trauma seems to seize one up. I can never go when I'm visiting. Think of Dad. He comes home from New Zealand to go to the loo. Release of tension, you see. Some people don't go for days together and it's quite normal. Queen Victoria was always writing to her children about constipation and fresh air. Then Albert died from bad drains. Ironic.

They did a lot of research on it during the war because of lifeboats. I mean people didn't go for three weeks or more. When you come to think of it, just a bucket on a boat. Maybe not even a bucket.

I think the Navy is an authority on constipation. It was a naval doctor who wrote that book on bran. Let's have another try. If I put it in soup it wouldn't make you cough. Or if I squidged it up with All-Bran, cream and sugar?

I don't want you to get like Uncle Arthur wandering about in his pyjama jacket eating Ex-Lax.

———————

An Indian with a strong Welsh accent has just come to read the gas meter.

I put the bed mat on the lawn because I felt it couldn't stand being on the line while still wet. Some of the stitching is very rotten. It'll be an enormous task mending it, darling, but I'll bring the bag of bits and it'll be something to do while you are sitting.

Boot was sick again, but very neatly, and there was a little patch of fur in the middle so maybe the vet was right after all.

———————

Sorry I didn't tell you about the dentist. I thought you looked a bit bleak when I got home. Forgot. Sorry. Of course, I was late leaving and I couldn't find my keys. (They were on top of the fridge.) Then I lost my handbag. (I'd put it down by the front door.) I didn't have time to come up.

I was running down Fawley Road when I noticed something odd about my left leg. A certain stiffness about the knee. I slowed down a bit and walked briskly on, thinking bleakly about old age. It wasn't till I was sitting on the tube that I noticed a dingy clump of cotton sticking out of my left trouser leg. I tried to pretend it was perfectly normal to pull a pair of knickers out of my trouser leg and push them into my handbag.

I once dropped my handbag on the tube whereupon it burst open and scattered a packet of Tampax all over the floor in front of a large class of small boys from that posh prep school in Hampstead.

———•—

Do you think we should manufacture a pocket on your pinny a little higher up? For the aid, I mean. When you sat down at lunch it was under the table. You'll have to bring it out and lay it down, trying always to have the little round speaker bit facing upwards – or outwards if it is clipped on to your pinny, and I think above waist level. ('Where is that?' you cry.) Up the 'orspital they said you might hear swishing noises from some materials you wear, and some fabrics crackle.

It worked best at tea, didn't it? I didn't raise my voice one little bit. If you sit there holding it towards me it works a treat. A carpeted room and no extraneous noise or fidgeting members of the public.

I don't think Sanatogen can make you dizzy. Were you bending down a lot? Looking at Boot? I know. I agree. There is a decided swelling.

Hurrah for Pooh.
For who? For Pooh!

Tremendous celebrations downstairs. Dad did a rather undignified dance from study to wine rack and will propose your health at supper tonight.

Sausages and mash.

I was so thrilled to see you beaming away all pink and pretty that I will not even impose sanctions on whoever smuggled in the Ex-Lax.

PS If I stew a large bowl of Bramleys to serve with the All-Bran, will you promise me not to take Ex-Lax every night?

Matron

He says it's cancer, darling, and he can't operate. I shall tell the girls at teatime. We'll probably come up to your room. Dad has gone to golf to stride about.

I went up to Flax's and bought a packet of smoked-salmon bits. He can't say how long she has left, but he gave her an injection of steroids and vitamins, which will give her a terrific boost and we should see a difference in her within twenty-four hours. She may even meet you tomorrow morning as of old, so take care on the landing.

She liked the smoked salmon.

See you at tea.

Well, onwards and upwards, darling. I may try and clean shed out tomorrow if weather contin-ues fine. If not, I may do out china cupboard. I did floors very thoroughly last week, so if you do waist-level dusting, I'll just come behind you with the polisher.

Notes to my mother-in-law

waist level dusting

Fish and chips takeaway? Haddock? Or, I know, what about *skate* if they have it? I'll just get one portion of chips and two of whatever we decide on because that will give us spare for Boot and batter for the birds.

———

I was sitting at the kitchen door in the last of the sun this evening doing the crossword when Boot came out and walked up to the end of the garden. The melancholy slowness of her walk struck me to the heart. She sat down, curled her tail round her body as neatly as ever she did and stared into the shadows. I put down my paper and called to her gently, and she turned and stared at me in an abstracted sort of way, and then when I held out my hand she moved towards me with the shadow of an old hope in her eyes, touched my hand with her dry hot nose and sat down on the crossword. That cheered me up.

Do you remember how we lost her not five minutes after we brought her to the house, and how wild with grief the children were and how even you wept till we found her in the cutlery drawer?

Do you remember how she used to live under our bed in order to occupy it when we left? Em used to call to her severely, 'Come out of there, Boot. I see your boiling eyes.'

Nor will I ever forget when she had her kittens in the bottom drawer of the wardrobe and I lay on the floor and held her hand. And Dad woke the RSPCA at two in the morning to tell them his cat was having a breech birth as all we could see were three tiny paws sticking out of her hindquarters.

And do you remember when we moved house I slept on a mattress in the sitting room to try and prevent her escaping up the chimney?

Of course, that's when we discovered she could get out through the letter-box. So she was lost for two days and nights and we fed her poor children every two hours – or was it four? – with an eye-dropper. On the third night we heard her call in the garden and Dad fed the kittens outside so she slowly came nearer, tortured by their squeaks. After that she was fine.

I always wish I'd never had her 'doctored'. When she came home with that bandage round her middle, looking humiliated and aggrieved, I was stricken with guilt. She wouldn't look at me. There ought to be a pill they could take. Animals, I mean. Mother had a medical acquaintance who fed birth-control pills to pigeons to keep the numbers down.

Oh, Boot. We've never seen eye to eye, have we, till just these last weeks. What a successful, controversial cat you've been. I'm glad you were wicked and nicked Gran's fresh crab.

So there we sat in the sun and communed one with another and sighed over lost summer times.

I don't think we'll have her with us till Christmas, will we?

———

You are sound asleep, thank heaven, but I have put your drink on the table in case you wake. The yellow pill in the spoon beside it should be taken if you are in any pain at all. I'll leave the landing light on, just in case, and our door is open. Have put bell by wireless. Don't hesitate to use it.

We are all so relieved that you are home. How you did it without breaking something I will never know. The noise was tremendous. Like three loads of laundry with boots on. And it was followed by this eerie silence when Virginia and I sat open-mouthed with eyebrows in our hair.

The ambulance men (one was a girl, did you notice?) told me you shouldn't have been wrapped up so warmly. I always thought you had to keep the patient warm. I forget what they said now, of course, but it's something to do with bringing the blood too near the surface of the skin, which would be foolish if you needed an operation or anything, which, of course, was why I didn't give you any tea, darling. I felt such a cow. And you were just coming downstairs for a cup too. Bet you were parched. Also, I didn't come with you in the ambulance because I couldn't have got home again in time for the girls. So there you were with a cushion under your head and your feet in the air saying you were sorry. I found your other shoe under the hallstand, but I can't find your deaf-aid anywhere.

Not surprisingly, I forgot the gingerbread so the edges are all black but the middle is surprisingly edible, if a bit chewy, so we just sat and ate it out of the tin. I'll have to soak the edges off.

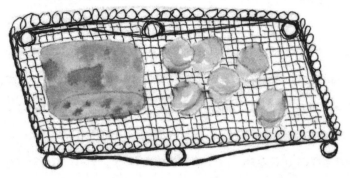

horrid gingerbread & nice scones

Your specs flew off and you landed on them so one of the legs is a bit bent. Dad has been trying to straighten them over the gas, but he's a bit tentative so I'll take them round to the oculist tomorrow.

But I'm amazed you didn't smash something. There's only a little chip on the hallstand and at least this time you weren't wearing two pairs of bloomers. Remember when you broke your leg in Scotland and you had put on two of absolutely everything for fireworks? That little Indian doctor had rather a testing time cutting you out of your drawers. He probably thought it was an ancient Scottish custom.

There is a bit of a bump on the side of your forehead, which will probably show up more tomorrow. You must have biffed your head on the banisters. Nurse thought you may get a black eye. Ooh. Gorgeous.

I'll just prop this up against the clock in case you wake. Take the yellow pill, darling.

Didn't they use to put a raw steak on a black eye? Why?

———·—

Well done, Gran. You will find the yellow pill on spoon beside glass of soda water. Here are a few wine gums beside them. Hand bell by wireless. I've moved the flowers in case they get knocked over.

I'll ask Nursie about Benecol tomorrow. I know you have great faith in it but I think we'd better not take it till we know if it mixes with everything else.

I do wonder what it's made of. I simply cannot get it out of the carpet whatever I do, and I was scrubbing away the other day when I suddenly saw that the pattern on the edge has a line of helmeted warriors doing unmentionable things to each other. I had no idea it was so bellicose. Anyway, I've rubbed a couple of warriors threadbare and the Benecol is still clinging to the warp or the woof or the weft or whatever you call it – it's like paint.

Dad wants to know who is going to wash his knickers while his mum is confined to barracks. He chipped most of the gingerbread out of the tin and ate it. The mangled tin is soaking in the wash-house sink.

I enjoyed cleaning the stained-glass window.
It's come up lovely so it has. I think the landing
might seem brighter now, and the stair-rods are
all fixed and firm. You know the rose you gave
me from the Harrods flower show? The 'Pink
Grootendorst' it's called, poor thing. Well, it's
flourishing over on the other side of our fence,
but it looks half dead this side. Rather hurtful.
I saw this while hanging out of the window, so
I sloshed all my soapy water over the bad bits
and missed. Half the bucketful hit the deck and
half went down that shiny new pipe sticking out
of next door's side wall. I think I've flooded
their central-heating system. When the doorbell
went a while later I assumed it was next door
come to complain. And there they were. I took
a deep breath and started to apologize, but
they'd only called to show us their new baby.
Brought it up to see you but you'd dropped off.
Nice little person no bigger than a thermos and
very comfy in a carry-bag. I shut up about the

central-heating. If I've wrecked it they'll only find out in September.

———•••———

Mrs Wilson says she was nearly cremated this week. Mr Wilson filled her cigarette lighter too full, she says, and the flames shot up so high it set her spectacles on fire. She managed to throw them off but they were burning the carpet so she had to pick them up with fire tongs and put them in the sink. She says the smell was frightful.

I can't understand how her hair didn't catch fire. She uses masses of hair lacquer and it's very combustible.

'It's the absolute bitter end in whiskers,' she said.

Boot actually had a boxing match with Dad tonight.

He has put a cardboard box lined with a

cushion and his copy of the Times by the kitchen heater.

Guess what? You will squeal. I got up this morning to investigate an odd sound. A cross between castanets and a kettle coming to the boil. I thought it was the central heating, so I felt the radiators in our room and thought, That's it. They're tepid at the top so they probably need milking or bleeding or whatever it's called. Wandered to the bathroom and the noise followed me onto the landing. Went to the loo and it stopped. It got very loud suddenly when I went near the laundry basket so I emptied it out in case there was something lurking in a pocket. Nothing. (Well, one ½d bit.) Opened my drawer to get some clean knickers and while I was struggling them on the noise got rather aggressive. Sat on the bed nonplussed and scratched my head. There it was. There it was. The noise, I mean, the rattling about. I'd run out of curlers last night and I'd used a tube of Anadin with six pills in it on my fringe and jammed it into place with two bent hairpins. It's done the trick with the curl, I think you'll find.

PS Do you remember the night I swallowed my moustache bleach?

Went to get our Friday fish this afternoon and told our bespectacled friend about Boot. He had wondered about all that smoked salmon. Goodness, he is nice. I think you might have to be nice to be a fishmonger. Carpenters are nice. Do they start nice or is it the job? Anyway, Spectacles was the one who said to drown your crab. I thought this sounded idiotic but he said, 'No. Drop it upside down into warm water and wait till it stops bubbling.' Help. It's time you were up. If the water is too hot he says the crab will 'shoot its claws' (as in gents shooting their shirt cuffs). He and his wife are very keen on amateur theatricals and he was a virgin when he married. I didn't enquire about his wife.

My uncle Charlie announced one New Year's Eve that he was a virgin. You should have heard the aunts. They shrieked. He wasn't a proper uncle or they would have known. Not quite sure how he got to be uncled. Anyway, he was a private in World War I and in his first week at the front he dropped his rifle in the mud and ruined it. His commanding officer shouted a lot and he was ordered to steal one from the next dug-out, which he did. And then he sat about for so long in the mud that the seat of his trousers rotted, so he stuck a tin biscuit lid inside them for protection. 'I always took it out on fine days,' he said, 'in case it caught the sun and a sniper took aim.'

Father said that the Cameron Highlanders were ordered to muddy their spats because they were a dazzling white target for the Hun. Within 24 hours the order was countermanded by the Big Chief Cameron of Lochiel who presumably didn't want his Highlanders to look slovenly when dead.

But I digress. Poor young Charlie came a cropper on his first bombardment. It was what he called a whizz-bang bomb, which sounds rather fun but wasn't. You had to judge the direction it was coming from and he ran the wrong way.

I think he lost his crown jewels, the whole arrangement. His voice stayed deep enough but it hardly compensates.

———

Glad you liked the pudding. We made it with 'foozle'. This was my granny's favourite. You

"Foozle"

boil a tin of Carnation milk – not condensed, Carnation. I think for about ten minutes or so. At least until the label comes off. Then it whizzes up into a dropping-cream consistency.

I remember watching horrified as Granny poured it over her salad. I dared not utter. She ate it with relish and declared it delicious. I think she had it with her pudding as well. We all used to leave the disgusting cooking sherry at the bottom of the trifle Flora made and Granny would polish it off. She never would have done so had she known it was the demon alcohol. She always poured every dreg in bottle or glass into the rose-bowl on the dining table.

Someone who shall be nameless has put bubble gum on the dresser and lifted the veneer.

Bit of an atmosphere downstairs.

Ta-ra!

———•——

Darling, I can't believe you heard them! It was two hedgehogs. Dad put out a tin plate of bread and milk when he saw the first one. I told him milk was bad for them but he didn't believe me. Nor would the hedgehogs. When the second one turned up there was an ugly scene, followed by vigorous sex on the tin plate. Imagine. All those prickles. How do they manage? We were agog. I do hope it was a successful union.

Sex on a tin plate

Now it's raining and Dad has given them his golf umbrella.

———————

This will make you shriek. Mrs Wilson made little portions of chicken chasseur in plastic pots neatly sealed with clingfilm and put them in the deep freeze for Mr Wilson whilst she was away in 'orspital for her cataract operation.

Mr Wilson just put them in the oven as they were and ate the lot – pots and all. He's rather ill.

Not sure what it is, Gran. I think the chasseur bit is a cream sauce of some sort. Not your scene, I know.

———‑•‑———

Well, it's tragic downstairs. Boot is to go to the vet tomorrow. She will get an injection and he says she will just slip away. Em will take her, she wants to. Oh dear.

The banging you heard this evening was Dad removing the cat flap and boarding the hole up against the draught. He waited tactfully till Soph had gone out, which was quite funny as she scoured all Boot's dishes and hid them behind the shed while *he* was out. She is to plant them up, she says.

There will be a short ceremony in the garden at a later date. You will be advised.

It seems there is a new deaf-aid on the market. I keep seeing it. It's like an Alice band so you wear it on your head with these wee muff things that sit on your ears. Very practical. You'd be surprised how many young people are wearing them. You are not alone. I shall do a bit of research and report back, because I think they might be the very thing.

———·———

Darling, please don't worry. I'm sure it's just the bruising. Nursie said it was very severe. You were X-rayed upside down and sideways so they would be bound to see if the joint was loose. It's a big thing, like a light bulb and I think it's made of stainless steel.

Your specs are looking as good as new. The optician says they were all squinty and he thinks you've been taking them off by one leg. He says lift them off carefully in the middle on the bridge of your nose, or with both hands. Do you see what he means? He didn't charge by the way. Nice man. Says he'll come round to see you and maybe devise a padding for the specs so they won't clank about on your hearing-aid.

Talking of which! I told Dad about the new deaf-aid on the market and he tells me it's a thing called a Walkman which plays music into your ears. He and the girls were hysterical. Trust me to get it wrong!

———·—·———

It's a 'Zimmer', darling. A 'zither' is a musical instrument. Could come in useful for airing things, Dad says. Give it a go. It's a help to get to the loo at least, and awfully useful for getting out of bed if I leave it just beside you, pointing in the right direction. You can really lean on it. I do see that your mattress is a bit squashy and difficult to lift off. I wonder if we could put a board under it? My old drawing board might do. We'll try it.

Your black eye has gone a lovely yellow colour now with a tasteful purple swelling near your nose. Can you see? I expect it will slip downwards shortly since you are sitting up so much more. Very attractive. Mother always keeps 2 cotton-wool pads soaked in witch hazel on the top shelf of the fridge and recommends old cold teabags and slices of cucumber, but I don't think we can cope with such frippery. You hate the smell of witch hazel too, I seem to remember.

What made you think of Xmas? Good grief. Don't worry for the moment. I suspect we'll spend it at home this year anyway. I'd love to go up for New Year and you might be ready for the Dashing White Sergeant by then. You and Uncle Arthur. Can't you see it?

Actually, he used to be a bit of a lounge lizard. All those medals he keeps were for ball-room dancing, in particular the foxtrot, the two-step and the tango. (What is the two-step, by the way?) He would gallantly take me on to the floor at New Year celebrations and I'd be clamped firmly to his chest and his down below bits, which made me shriek and I always got calamine lotion over his suit. My back was covered in acne and Mother would try and cover it up, as my dance frock was a ghastly floral creation with a bathing-costume top made of stretchy elastic. Uncle Arthur would plonk his hot hand on my back and leave a full imprint. Oh, the shame!

Nor could I ever remember the moves in the eightsome reel, so Uncle Arthur would yank me around and everyone else would shout insults. Isn't growing up ghastly?

———

Mrs Keith

I loved New Year in Glasgow when I was home from school, especially when old Mrs Keith came. She was a tiny little person, terribly crippled by arthritis, and we adored her. She sat by the fire in the sitting room for all her meals and we would beg to be allowed to serve her. Best was to take in her tiny glass of sloe gin, which she held in her little paws so gently to sip, and under her skirts were huge black-patent pumps with a flat grosgrain-ribbon bow. Her wee feet were so bumpy and bent her shoes had to be big as boats. She was out of Dickens, really. I have very dim memories of old Mr Keith who was a little hunchback of a sweet soul with a huge red nose like Mr Punch. He used to keep a warehouse by the docks in Greenock or Paisley or somewhere, and they always had donkeys, parakeets, monkeys and other strange animals sent from abroad. I can't tell you why. I seem to think they were in quarantine. Mother said some bizarre foreign bird arrived at the warehouse and started to moult, and of course being winter by the docks, it would be damp and cold so little Mrs Keith knitted it a sort of woollen body stocking. She made herself little woollen mittens and turned heels

bizarre foreign bird

and all such. Bad for the arthritis is knitting I'm
told, so beware.

Mending our patchwork quilt would be all
right tho', wouldn't it? Hint. Hint.

Well, we went to Scotland for New Year. Of course we did. We took the patchwork with us. Our journey was meticulously planned. We rose early and Gran took no tea. The glove compartment was closely packed with egg sandwiches, Maynard's wine gums, several bananas, one orange and any milk left in the fridge.

Forton was our favoured stop on the M6. We ignored the bridge café and drove straight to the petrol station, which had a loo with a ramp easily negotiable on a zimmer frame. When Gran was comfortably returned to the car, she would give me some of her pension to buy my coffee, chocolate raisins and liquorice allsorts for pudding.

In our first years together things had been very different. We went by sleeper on the Royal Scot, smuggling Boot, then a kitten, into our carriage where she slept on my face. In later years she was weighed on the platform and given a ticket. Mostly she travelled with us in the car and threw up, howling, at Stafford.

The train was a triumph. The ferry crossing was a nightmare. To Gran, it was sheer insanity to travel on water. Long years before, her first sweetheart had gone to Canada to seek his fortune and sent her a ticket so that she could join him. She refused. She couldn't face the ocean crossing. Her father went instead. I got the impression that he did rather well, but when he was travelling home, in steerage, the weather was fierce. He caught bronchitis, kept it, and died.

So started Gran's long life in service, often in and around London for I know she saw Zeppelins during World War 1. They came over on moonlit nights and seemed so low she felt she could put out her hand and touch them.

Then she was a cook in a country hotel where she fell in love with the waiter – there was only one. Every Friday she cooked an omelette for a gentleman who called on his motorbike. It was T. E. Lawrence. She called him Mr Ross. 'He loved my omelettes,' she said.

On that very first ferry crossing, it was only the rumour of a school of dolphins that persuaded Gran to open her eyes, squeezed tight shut against drowning. By a rare miracle the water was satin smooth. She didn't see the dolphins. She saw the hills.

And then she saw the cottage. Her old rose, 'New Dawn', was overwhelming the tiny porch, creeping under the gutters and shifting the slates.

Everything enchanted her, even the weather – even the outside loo. We all spent too long in there, with the door open wide to the view: a local seal spent early mornings perched on a flat rock, like a slice of melon.

Milk was delivered daily in a can by the gate and smelt of cows. Gran liked to fetch the *Sunday Post* herself from the tiny post office next door and chat to Mrs Gardener, the postmaster's wife, who played the violin on Burns night with her back to the audience.

And then there was Gertie Mackay who sat at her door on a lobster pot and waylaid Gran on her way to the village tea rooms and fresh pancakes. They shared stories about their life in service. In Gertie's day it had been customary to clean the house mercilessly for Hogmanay. 'Seven washing waters and vinegar in the final rinse,' said Gertie.

The kids would fill pails with mussels and winkles from the shore and Dad would catch buckets of mackerel, bringing them home on a string for Gran to gut and fry. Once he got a fish hook embedded in his hand and fainted. 'He doesn't get that from me,' she said.

For serious shopping we went to 'town', stocking up on essentials like potato scones, mutton pies and 'squashed-fly cemeteries', a particularly appealing fruit slice. In summer there was rhubarb ice-cream, and in winter the best fish and chips on the coast. 'Town' was Dunoon, voted the 'top resort in Scotland'.

A decent whisky and top snacks were always kept for first-footers at Hogmanay but this time we didn't go to the fireworks. Not in the dark on a zimmer frame. Some years before we had set out for the party on a frosty night when the sky was crusty with stars but no moon. We had just waltzed down the path to the little gate, from which steps led to the road, when I ran back to fetch a decent torch and Gran, launching herself into the darkness, fell onto the road and broke her thigh. That was when the young Indian doctor had to cut her out of her double bloomers.

I was only too pleased to use Gran as an excuse to go to bed with lights out before the dreaded midnight hour when ships hooted at each other on the Clyde.

New Year's Eve supper had been classic. Mother had made a creamy rice mould for one pudding, decorated with grated pistachio nuts. With a mouthful of ham, Uncle Arthur suddenly shouted: 'That pudding is moving!' The pistachios were walking about. Mother had kept them for years and they were full of weevils. Sophie says Mother's fridge is like a scientist's laboratory.

The cold and damp always affected what Gran would call her 'war wounds'. She used to say she had discovered Scotland too late and quite often came to breakfast saying she had been wandering the hills all night. On one of our early summers we took her up the hill we called 'Boiled Egg Bump', since it was perfect for picnics. She just had a bit of difficulty coming down.

'It's the same on Everest,' Dad said.

Lately, and unsurprisingly, the war wounds had troubled Gran more than usual. One doctor thought she might have broken a rib sneezing. But she hadn't sneezed. On our long, wistful journey home she was quiet and uncomplaining but it was clear that it pained her very much coming out of what she called her 'stuck sitting' position.

I was concerned. Safely upright and on her zimmer frame she said of the pain: 'It'll go the way it came.'

Apologies, darling, for such a late cuppa. I locked myself OUT. My keys were in my jacket pocket and I'd just shoved my coat on over my nightie to go to Mistry's and get some milk. (The kids made cocoa last night.) Climbed over the back gate with great difficulty. Made a pile of those bricks left over from the front path and that gave me a boost. Hoisted me and milk up and sat astride the gate rather painfully, plucking up courage to throw myself into the yard, having tossed the milk into that lavender bush by the water butt. Slid down the back door ripping nightie on the bolt and hoping against hope that the kitchen door might be open. It wasn't. Peered in all the windows in the faint hope of help. Sat on the back step and swigged some milk miserably.

Then I remembered the plot of a rather famous French film called 'Rififi' or something, where robbers used an umbrella to catch a key. I just used a sheet of your Daily Mail I found in the dustbin. I pushed this under the door below the keyhole. Then I found, after much fossicking, a peculiarly strong twig, which I pushed into the keyhole, wiggling it about to dislodge the key, which I could just see by leaning against the door and squinting thru the glass. It took ages but, to my joy, the key finally dropped on to the paper, which I tenderly withdrew and, lo!, I unlocked the door and put the kettle on. Rather damp, scratched and torn, with a button off my coat (yes, please), but what a TRIUMPH.

Do you remember that nice policeman who got into my Volkswagen Beetle with a coat-hanger? He wouldn't let me watch.

———·———

I don't know if they cremate cats. I should have asked. Do you think we'd get her ashes in a tiny urn? I've kept her flea collars and her bell.

There was a chap in Ma's village called Gully Wishart who had so many cats he wore flea collars on his wellingtons.

We'll have Boot's short memorial service soon and plant something. Cat mint? Does it repel or attract? I've never known.

Mrs Wilson has asked to be scattered along the path she takes to the tennis courts. Arnold says his uncle Clem wanted to have his ashes scattered off Blackpool pier, but Auntie Blanche thought they would get blown back all over people so she only took his teeth. Even that was a bit dodgy, she said.

Wait till you hear this. Mother had Miss Delmahoy to tea. Do you remember her? She used to be Matron at a big hospital in Glasgow and she has retired to a bungalow across the way next door to Mrs Moffat. It is she who has that fantastic garden, and Mother is desperate to pick her brains. Mrs M says Miss D gardens with a big silver-plated serving spoon and tells stories of the amount of cardboard coffins she had to order and store for World War II. She's known besides for doing intricate tapestry work called Richelieu, using fine black and gold thread, and she keeps it on a frame like a music stand, covered in muslin when she isn't working on it, rather like old Queen Mary waiting for her carriage. She used to make stair-carpets, Queen Mary did. I once saw an example displayed at the English Speaking Union in Berkeley Square. Bet she had help.

Well, anyway, Ma was determined to do things properly so she unpacked the tea-set from the dining-room dresser and washed it tenderly, checking everything for chips in case of GERMS. She even bleached the inside of the teapot with a touch of Domestos. She got a large carton of whipping cream from Ross's Dairies in Dunoon to serve with fresh scones and this year's bramble jelly. Perfect. Miss D duly arrived. She always ignores the bell, knocks peremptorily (is that a word?) and walks straight in. Then it transpired that she takes lemon in her tea so there was a bit of a kerfuffle while Ma looked for a lemon and could only find half of a rather old squashed one in the fridge, and then she couldn't concentrate on anything because she was sure the tea tasted of bleach. Miss D talked all the time, which made it easier. It was only after they had toured the garden and Miss D had departed that Ma found her tea-plate with her napkin delicately covering most of her uneaten scone. Ma had been in such a flap that she had taken the wrong carton out of the fridge and served the warmed scone with cottage cheese instead of Jersey cream.

baby elephant?

Uncle Arthur said the tea was disgusting. Ma says there's no way she'll sleep tonight.

———

Gran, it's remarkable. I've never seen your skin so clear. You must be thrilled. D'you think it's because of this enforced rest? Posh people with psoriasis spend pots of money and rush off to the Dead Sea, which sounds alarming, but I understand bathing in its salty water is very efficacious. I'd have thought it was agony getting salt into those raw patches, but it's bordering on miraculous and apparently you can float on the surface reading a newspaper. Something to do with the salt. You simply can't sink. The Adriatic is pretty salty. I couldn't get my bottom under the water. Dad said it looked as if I was being followed by a baby elephant. Or a small island.

You are still taking the gloop, aren't you? Or did we stop it? Whatever. I think it's the total rest. But while you are sitting up for lunch or tea, please remember to waggle your ankles, toes pointing up! Toes pointing down! And then round and round as demonstrated by Nursie. Life is not all beer and skittles.

Matron

Where's your clean nightie, Gran? He's coming to see you tomorrow after surgery. When I told him there was this blobby thing next to your sternum (posh name for your breastbone) he was thrilled and asked if I was a nurse. Maybe even a doctor? I said, no, but I was sure I could deal with the blob very neatly before tea. It's just like an ounce of suet, I said, no bigger than a baby's bootee and just under the skin. A quick snip and that's that. He said perhaps not. Ooh, I'd love to do it. It wouldn't take a minute and, after all, I had my tonsils taken out on the dining-room table.

It's not a generally known fact but I did intend to become a doctor. Don't laugh. Do you remember during the war there were huge posters warning people about VD? In Glasgow they were everywhere. Aunt May said it meant Digging for Victory but I could read the small print. Besides, they were on the back of every public loo door so that you could read all the details from a perched position. I made under-cover enquiries in a luridly illustrated medical dictionary I found in Granny's bookshelves only to discover that I had all the symptoms listed and would surely die young and in disgrace. My best friend Isobel Hebblethwaite said you could catch it from loo seats so when I stayed with her I used to pee in the sink. Realising I was socially unacceptable, the obvious career move was to sacrifice myself for the human race and maybe work with lepers in the Gorbals.

Oops, there's the phone.

That was Mother. Everything much as usual. Yesterday she found Uncle Arthur buttoned and belted into his raincoat. Lying on the sofa head back, mouth open, specs squint, teeth dangling. She thought he was dead and went to phone the surgery. Just as the doctor answered Uncle Arthur shouted, "He owes me £1."

she thought he was dead

I think the doctor is the only well-dressed man ever to darken our door. He even wears a waistcoat. Thank God we tidied your bedroom. Of course, when he rang the doorbell I was creaming butter and sugar with that electric whizzer thing you gave me and the bell startled me so that I lifted it out of the bowl without turning it off and covered the walls with gobbets of cake mix. Typical. I thought he was coming after *evening* surgery.

Anyway, he seemed delighted to view the baby's bootee and not unduly worried about anything except what he describes as your "pallor". What does he expect? It's not much fun baring your bosom to young men in mid-morning. However, he will be in touch shortly as he is going to send us to a friend of his in the 'orspital who, he says, is top man for bumps and awfully nice. He will make the appointment, he says, and hopes to let us know within the week. Huh, we'll see.

I'm off to put the kettle on and clear the kitchen. Back with cuppa shortly. Well done, Gran. You were brilliant.

PS Can we watch the snooker up here with you tonight?

———

Just in case we get called to the hospital within a week or so, let's get your hair done. Tracey can come on Thursday, and backwards over the sink is all right now, isn't it? I'll bring up that kitchen chair.

Dixon of Dock Green
or
This is your Life

I think your best blouse is in the laundry bag still. I'll wash it today. Don't laugh. I will, and I'll hang out the tweed pinny with the zip. You don't want to have to pull anything over your head. Actually, your stays will be difficult for a doctor to negotiate. Can you use garters for your stockings? We'll take a wheelie for the endless corridors and you'll be sitting down for the viewing. Maybe your bloomers will keep your stockings up, if you are sitting down. That's if the elastic is tight enough.

Reminds me of old Mrs Hatrick up the glen who had a thing about spiders. She says she saw their teethmarks in the butter and used elastic bands to tighten the legs of her bloomers because she thought spiders would invade.

Remember Boot eating spiders and throwing up over your bedcover? We will discuss and unravel the garter problem tonight.

My drawing board is under your mattress, so can we bring the old card table into your room? The aim is to finish the jigsaw before you go in for the boob job. It might be quite fun and any visitor can wander in and add a piece here and there. Dad says if we rearrange the furniture a bit we can get it all set up under the window and you can have your chair beside it. Hurrah.

———

Gran's room had always been a storeroom with a bed in it. She welcomed this sort of interference and she loved it when we watched the snooker lying on her bed, the only available space in the room other than her big armchair. In its heyday Gran's cottage must have had elastic sides. It was home for one husband for a bit, three sons, one daughter, an elderly mother, an elderly dog and, during the war, a floating population of evacuees. Anything that interfered with the general flow was thrown higgledy-piggledy into Gran's little bedroom at the top of the narrow stairs. Problem solved.

After the war, things thinned out. One by one the boys left home and eventually she shared the cottage with her daughter, her daughter's husband and their small son, who was the apple of Gran's eye. We used to take our girls to stay or just visit for treat weekends. I remember with awe the massive teas served on a spotless lace-edged tablecloth. The children, their noses level with the table top and eyes on the cake, equally awed, behaved like angels. No, not the jam tarts quite yet. Bread and butter first. There was always a bag of Mixed Assortment to be handed round when we watched Gran's favourite *Dixon of Dock Green* in the front room.

Then one summer Gran was due into London from a visit to her eldest son who lived abroad, and I was to put her on the train home to Horsham. I think I was washing up when the phone went. It was her son-in-law ringing from the cottage. 'Is she there?' he asked.

'No! She isn't expected till three fifteen,' I said.

'My wife,' he said. 'The drawers are empty and the wardrobe is full of hangers.'

Gran's daughter had run away to Cornwall with a beautiful young man, taking her little son with her.

I made up a bed and a thermos of hot, sweet tea. I told Gran in the car that I was going to take her home to our place at least for a night and I told her why. She took the news, mug in hand, with surprising equanimity. I drank most of the tea.

Years later, I learnt that Gran had helped pack up her daughter's clothes for her flight. Not many moons later she packed up her own and came to us.

It occurs to me that we ought to cut your nails before D-Day. I don't think they do that sort of thing in 'orspital. You can soak your feet while jigging and sawing and we'll use Dad's clippers.

Let's watch Delia Smith tonight?

———

We've lost the lid of the jigsaw, so we will have to struggle without looking at the picture. It's not so much the ship, it's all that blue of sky and sea.

I've checked the elastic in your bloomers and I think they'll be fine. It was Granny who used to wear wee garters of black elastic on her enormous knee-length bloomers. They were an unfortunate green, which seemed to glow in the dark. When she went walk-about guests were horrified to be confronted by a small bald ghost wearing plus-fours. She left her bunch of false curls on the dressing-table after nine at night when she was on patrol before bed and on her way to turn the electricity off at the mains. She said she had a degree in electricity. Her gnashers were kept in a bedside jug, tho' quite often they rattled about in her bed-jacket pockets among 'sneesh paper' and charcoal biscuits. She left a trail everywhere she went like Hansel and Gretel and me with hairpins.

Yes, I know, I'm frightful about Granny but she was such a thundering old bigot. If nuns called

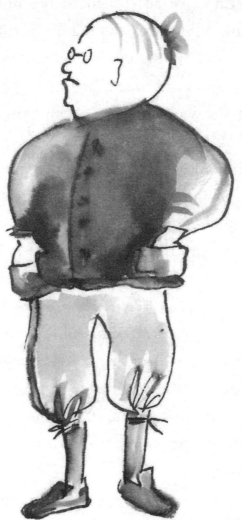

unfortunate green bloomers

collecting, we all rushed to the door before Granny, as she was a miniature version of Ian Paisley and quite as loud. Once she had shouted about the Pope being an instrument of the devil, she would play wobbly hymns on the piano and sing off-key in an uncertain soprano.

I did enjoy sitting with her in 'the morning room' when she read the paper breathing heavily and peering thru a large magnifying glass. With any luck you might get a bit of chocolate from her bureau drawer. She would prise out the soft centre with one of her hair-pins, eat it, return the hairpin to her bun, and hand me the chocolate shell. Sometimes she gave me the Russian Toffee because that stuck to her dentures, but I found her careful concentration and her clicking teeth rather soothing.

PS My specs were found under the washing line when I stepped on them. They must have fallen off when I pinned up your blouse.

———

Mother sends much love. She is fed up. Uncle Arthur has been very mumpish. Mrs Mac sent round some lovely home-baked ham studded with cloves and he complained bitterly that 'Mrs Mac might be all very well, but her ham was full of nails.'

He won't eat Ma's mashed potato either and asked for the stuff in a packet called Smash. 'No lumps,' he said.

———

Talking of which, there is movement on the lump front. We are to go on Friday next at 11.15 a.m., which is wonderfully much sooner than expected tho' I don't like the look of that '15' detail. Can he be seeing people every 15 minutes? We'll take the Daily Mail, a pen and some wine gums. Thank Heaven we got your hair done.

It'll be nice to get it over before next week-end when we are all at home and a roast is planned. You may be allowed to recline with Room Service on Saturday and then you will be escorted downstairs to oversee the Yorkshire pudding department. What do I do wrong? Dad stuck my last efforts to the fridge door and is demanding 'the nun's farts' his mother makes.

———

Ooh, what about that surgeon? Wasn't he gorgeous? Long time since I've seen a bow tie. When he bent to pat you on your shoulder I thought he was going to kiss you.

'Half man, half woman,' he murmured admiringly.

I told him you had that boob off forty years ago and he was THRILLED. He said you were 'a miracle'.

Did you mind all those students having a feel? I was a bit worried and the surgeon said rather firmly they weren't to *squeeze* it. In medical terms it's known as a Mouse apparently.

Do you mind nurses calling you Annie? I felt you might.

Anyway, Mouse is to be removed and Mr McClure, the surgeon, is looking forward to it. All very well for him, I say, but he makes it sound easy and comfortably imminent.

———

I know tea was a bit peculiar, Gran, but Sophie was determined to impress. It's called Lamb Moroccaine or something. I can't explain why it was grey but the fingernails were actually flaked almonds. I shall waltz in later with your Sanatogen and the last of the cake.

———

Don't worry, Gran, we've got time, but let's make a list tomorrow. Where's your wee case? It used to be on top of the wardrobe. Lost? Talking of which – Mother couldn't find Uncle Arthur this morning when she took him his tea. He'd got into bed upside down. His head was where his feet should be if you follow me.

———

We'll use some of this baby talc to stop your legs sticking together.

I'll turn your radiator off in your room. It's horrid getting hot and sweaty because it makes you cold. Aunt Ella sweated so much at night she took a hair dryer to bed with her. She said it had nothing to do with the weather.

———

Right. Paper and pen at the ready. Let's make a list of requirements.

- talcum powder
- paper hankies
- 2 *good* hankies for handbag and pocket
- 2 nighties? One on and I bring a clean when needed?
- dressing-gown
- your sponge bag with –
  soap, facecloth, hairbrush and comb
- Steradent
- big tub psoriasis cream
- bottle of arthritis gloop
- those yellow pills
- handbag with purse with coins in for buying newspaper etc.
- Daily Mail
- pen and pencils
- book – I got you a Reginald Arkell at the library
- two pairs of specs and, last but not least, your hearing-aid. We might get help with that while you are in.
- Please tick list and add any other requirements.

Quite agree – I think Maynards wine gums essential. Well done.

———

Mother says she has discovered why the prize fuchsia overwinters so well. You will recall I know that Uncle Arthur won a prize for it at last year's flower show having bought it the day before at Marks & Spencer or was it Woolworths? Anyway, he has it in its pot just below the bedroom window and she caught him peeing on it.

Shades of the aunts, three of whom sat backwards out of an upstairs window and peed on a parishioner's flowery hat while she sat talking to their papa. I loved that story when I was little and even now I wish I'd known my grandpapa. He died rather young, and not surprising after Granny and eight children. Mother's memories of him are rare, but he used always to wear a

he peed on his first prize

velvet smoking jacket when he was at home, and if she cried in the night and he came to sit on her bed, she knew she would find a stick of nougat in his breast pocket.

I was about 9 when I got caught short in the ladies' compartment of the little local train to Wemyss Bay and boarding school. The train was corridor-less and loo-less, so I ate all the chocolates from a Christmas gift box, peed into it and threw the box out of the window just past Fort Matilda.

Your case was under the bed.

Dad has ascertained that wheelchairs are always available and he polished your shoes before he left.

No, darling. Manchester.

We'll cab it to the hospital as Dad has got the car.

In Manchester.

He has added a packet of Rich Tea biscuits to your luggage.

Your carriage is ordered for 10 a.m.

No, darling, he's in Manchester.

We will be very leisurely, and you won't be harassed by anyone. Mr McClure will visit you perhaps, but he's nice. Your case is packed and ready, outdoor clothing hanging up neatly by the airing cupboard.

You've got your nightie on back to front. That's tremendously good luck. Did you know?

———— · ————

The tall one in dark blue with the wee hat is a big sister. I think there aren't any Matrons any more. (She's very young, isn't she?) The pretty wee blonde in the pink stripes with the frilly hat is from Great Ormond Street and visiting or something. I miss all those daft wee organdie hats nurses used to wear. The staff nurses here look like hairdressers or checkout girls from Sainsburys.

The dark girl with bottle-top specs wearing a white coat is American or Canadian, I think, and very keen to interview you when you are available. She's doing a 'paper' or a dissertation or some such and she is fascinated by your interesting condition. One boob and a bump.

Don't know who is behind the curtains next door. No, it's not a man.

The young women opposite are a bit yellow, which is jaundice, I think. We both look very large and pink.

Am just disappearing to the loo for a minute. I can't go into the ward one. It's over there.

It wasn't far. Just outside the ward doors. Sister says you'll be done first in the morning. Expect to be wheeled off around 8 a.m. I forgot it's nil by mouth. There's a large notice behind your head.

I'm glad you get done first. You'll be back up by lunchtime and I'll be here about 3 p.m. to eat your grapes. You are a pretty sight sitting there. The nurses are mad about you already.

OK, sweetheart, I'm off. We shall take tea tomorrow together. I've just seen a trolley waltzing about.

Got everything?

Nurse has your medicaments.

Wine gums on your locker. Better ask if they're allowed.

They'll probably give you a pill to sleep. I hope so. It's a bit noisy behind the curtain.

No, it's a woman. The man is just visiting. Ta-ta.

Gran! I've left a wee notebook and a pen on your locker for nurses to write things in case you don't hear them.

———————

3.05 p.m. You are asleep, Gran! I'll be back later.

———•———

I've brought your post, Gran. It's like Christ-mas. Can't read this one. Who is Piggy? Your specs are in your handbag. Shall we do this later? I'll put them out on your locker. Don't think about it now.

I've started on your room. Found a desic-cated sock behind the radiator.

I took your clothes home yesterday and I'll bring you a clean nightie when needed. You are wearing a hospital gownie. The yellow ladies are looking better. How is the curtained lady?

Oh.

Isn't it quiet at the weekend? There will be no action till Monday. Is it painful just now, Gran? I'll tell Nursie. She'll want to know.

Will you eat any of this?

Let's ask for a cuppa and you can dunk a Rich Tea. I'll ask too if you can have a hot milk drink tonight. Horlicks or Ovaltine. Not chocolate. OK

I'll just give your specs a clean. Where's your hearing-aid? The family are coming up from Sussex to see you tomorrow so you will need it.

Gran, look. See this? It's your Visitors' Book. Get them to write in it.

It's absolutely pelting out there. I think I'll just get in beside you.

No, I came by cab. Dad has the car in Manchester.

You are tired. I'm going to go! I won't come tomorrow as everyone else is calling in. See you Monday. Not Dad. He's in Manchester. I'll see Sister before I go.

TTFN.

———·—

Ooh, get you, Annie Amelia. Tuppence to talk to you.

Big Sister and no less than three gorgeous doctors discussing your case across your bed. Could you hear what they were saying?

I longed to join in. They've all walked off looking important.

I've brought your post.

Your specs are on your nose.

I'll read the Visitors' Book.

You are to get an extra special X-ray tomorrow. They are concerned about your arthritis in the spine and it would be good to get that sorted while you're here. They aren't interested in your ears.

Sister says you are lovely. She'd like to keep you. Sounds as if you'll be coming home soon.

Yip. Yip.

———

Great excitement at home. Your room looks gorgeous already.

Sister says they'll send you home by ambulance and the hospital will loan us a bed-board and a monkey wrench.

That can't be right. No. Not a wrench. That's a tool of some sort, isn't it? No, this is something you can hang onto to lift yourself to a sitting position. The girls are particularly entranced by the scaffolding round the loo. It's spectacular. The loo is now a throne room.

Handles everywhere and a new battery in your wireless.

We won't all be at home when you get back, but I think that's quite good. It's always exhausting to travel and you need a few nights' good sleep. You will get a visit from Dr Thingummy and a nurse is to call to put on a new dressing.

Tunnocks Caramel Wafers are from Em and the Snowballs are from Soph. You'll be sick.

———

They gave her a year. She had a week. Almost her last words to me were 'I won't have any fish and chips tonight, darling.'

It was a Friday.

———•———

AFTERWORD

Notes from my daughters

'HOW'S GRAN?'

Jittery, at the end of a schoolday, but exhorted by my mother, I would take a deep breath and go up and lie on Gran's two-poster bed to – literally – bellow out the news of the day to her. I slightly dreaded it as it felt like hard work, but always ended up enjoying the time spent there and being pleased I had done it.

She was always 'Gran', never 'Grannie' – that was too cosy for her bony little shoulders and fingers gnarled into fists by arthritis. But there was nothing cosier than getting into her bed and being allowed to dunk an almost sweet Rich Tea biscuit into her early morning tea. In the corner of the top righthand drawer of her chest of drawers, which was a bit hard to pull out, there was always a paper poke of coconut logs dipped in chocolate, left there on purpose for her beloved little thieves. She was not one for hugs – she seemed physically unable, not unlike her daughter-in-law who still responds to embraces by folding up like a rather offended umbrella.

I remember presenting her for the first time to Stephen Fry and Hugh Laurie, who declared immediate and blind devotion both to her and her rock cakes. Stephen (who was twenty-one at the time) said she was lifted straight from the pages of Dickens, and a perfect Grandmother icon. 'How's Gran ?' they'd ask at the beginning of term and, to cries of great joy, I'd produce a tin of the spicy, crumbly misshapen buns made by Gran the day before, proud that her wartime baking went down so well with the young.

I opened the door to a policeman when I was what? – twelve? fourteen? – who, upon being informed that neither parent was in the house, proceeded to tell me that my Grandfather was dead. I thought he meant Grandad, my maternal grandfather, someone I loved because he always had sweeties in his pockets and smelt of pipe smoke. But, when Gran appeared beside my shuddering little body, it turned out to be her long-absent husband – someone I'd never met and knew nothing about. I didn't even know his name. Gran took over. I watched her face and saw no discernable reaction. I read a lifetime of stoic responses to challenges that would have floored many of us. A seminal moment, a moment by which to remember Gran, an image of a lifetime of suffering, strength and love.

Emma Thompson, 2011

DELUXE IN THE GRAN STAKES

Gran was there from when I can remember, until not very long before Dad died. She always had the room adjoining ours – first in the flat where I was born and then in the house with the unpainted wooden door and old brass handle.

Gran was Deluxe in the Gran stakes. She made all her dresses, which were cotton and floral — the one I can picture now was all 'Autumn Yellow and Browns'. She wore tights at the top end of their denier. Her teeth were by the bed in a fascinating pink fizz, and she seemed to wear an invisible hairnet. Her dear, hardworking hands were all whorls and worn, like something you might find on a beach. But sometimes I would spy on her from the stairs to see if she was pretending to be old. Perhaps, I thought, she would skip up those stairs when no one was looking. In the whispering wicker chair she would invariably have her 'Forty Winks'; I would press at her eyelids with my little fat fingers, and plead: 'Open your eyes! Open your eyes!'

Gran smelt of the Rich Tea biscuits that we would dip in Ovaltine, cuddled up together in her pillowy bed. She kept a smiley metal Toby jug on the chest of drawers – his hat was the lid and Gran had lined him with orange blotting paper and filled him with Wine Gums. I would often lift that hat, and pilfer those soft and favourite jellies. Sometimes there were 'Plain Janes' in his bulging waist-coat, brilliant oblong toffees with pink ribbon edges on the cellophane, and sometimes 'Richmond Selection', a curious confection of lemony centres in a thin butterscotchy case.

Gran made rock cakes every week (she always did me a special batch without peel). Sometimes she would make mutton stew with barley in it. It was erring on the grey and made me feel a bit sad and not very hungry. I didn't understand how poor she had been – she was in Service from the age of twelve.

My Uncle Fred was the son she had fought to keep when one of her employers made her pregnant. He wanted a child and his wife was barren. This was in 'The olden days'. I hope my darling Gran somehow really scared that man. I had no idea really about her Heart. My big sister asked questions as she got to be older, probing and engaged in the changing lot of women... I'm not sure I asked Gran anything at all. To grill her now of course would be a dream.

I remember being with Mum at The Royal Free Hospital as Gran died. She looked a bit worried and said 'Oh Phylli' and she closed her eyes and a trickle of blood came from her mouth. I thought I must be dreaming.

I must have seemed such a spoilt child sometimes with all that we had, but I know Gran Loved me very much and I knew I Loved her just the same.

Sophie Thompson, 2011